CREATING FIVE INCOME STREAMS FROM YOUR PRINTED

Learn How to Sell Your Printed Book and Make Money

CINDY HYDE

Guaranteed Success
if you use
the information
in this book.

Income
Stream
Number
One

Now What?

You've written a book! Congratulations! You have done something only a few ever do. You have released you creativity, your passion into the world! How did I know you wrote a book? Because you purchased this eBook.

If you are at this stage of the publishing your own book, you have figured out that books do not just sell themselves. If you are an Indie author like I am, Indie is a term created for those creative types like you and I who chooseto self-publish instread of going the traditional route, it means you are now in business for yourself. Unless of course you do not want to sell books except to your friends and family, and maybe a few others who happen to find your book by accident.

Books sell. That is a fact. According to Rosenthal (2011), $13.4 billion in sales were estimated by the US Census Bureau in 2012. Amazon itself, being one of the largest book retailers worldwide sold "nearly $11.0 billion in media during 2013."

Your book has just as much selling potential as any pther book written in your genre. Genre is your topic, subject, and your targeted audience. As long as it is on the same professional level and you promote (market and publicize) well, you can have as big of a piece of the book selling pie as you want.

Here are five things you need before you start making money:

1. Write something someone wants to read.
2. Write it to the best of your ability.
3. Make sure it is formatted correctly.
4. Get it edited by someone else. (Fiverr.com)
5. Create a great cover. Hire a graphic designer (Fiverr.com).

If you want your book to be competitive and make money your book has to compare to what is already on the market.

First Things First - Here's A Few Tips Before We Get to The Five Streams

The first thing you must do is write your book. Then you need to get it published. I take it you have made it that far already, if not, please see my other eBooks on Amazon.com. They will help you with the process and make things a little easier for you. I personally use Amazon's CreateSpace (createspace.com) because of all the benefits and of course the price is great! (No, I am not advertising for CreateSpace.com though it may seem like it. I am just sharing a good deal with you because I have experience with them and have had success so far. Besides the fact they make it simple to use and offer extras if I should need it. For a fee of course!

The very next thing you need to do, want to do, must do, is get people to read your printed book. You must get people to read your book if you ever want to make money from your book.

Let me tell you up front that the bulk of your money will be made by selling your book online. We will get to that part soon. For now, let's focus on creating your first income stream from your printed book. (Assuming you have your book in print. If not, then you will already know what to do when it does get printed.)

Income Stream Number One:
Sell to People You Already Know

The first income stream you can generate after you have your book in hand, or even before, is to sell to the people you already know. I say sell in the loosest term of the world. Everyone wants information. No one likes being "sold" something. So if you intend to sell your books to your friends and family, they will more than likely purchase your book because you have writtten one. Not because you sell it to them. My point is to inform them. Not sell them.

Letting people know about your book is all that is required for them. Let the people you know see what you have done. Many will celebrate with you. Many will even puchase your book. Don't expect high percentages. But expect purchases to be made.

The term "soft sell" mean anything to you? Advertise your book. Market your book. Promote your book. But the moment you start trying to sell your book you loose people's interest and some of them will even begin to avoid you because of it. Keep it simple. Keep it real.

One of the most powerful ways to sell books is to give them away. That's right. Give those books away. Many will pass them along after they have read them. This will get them interested in your next book. You are working on it right? Your next book should be in progress right now! Don't delay doing this valuable step to creating multiple income streams with one printed book. The more books you have... the more income streams you can create. So get busy and get started on that second book.

Tip: Always carry books with you in your vehicle or in your brief case or laptop case. You never know when you will run into someone who wants one of them.

Now, let's look at some ways to reach this group of people you already know.

Use the Platform You Already Have

The first way for you to make money with your printd book is to sell it to your friends, your family, your collegues, coworkers, and to all your social media contacts. You already have a group of readers that you can let know about your book.

They know you already but do they know you are wrting book? Let them know. Tell everyone! Hopefully they like you enough to read your book. The tip here is that the more readers you have the more books you will sell. You need to build a platform. A platform is a reader base. They are the poeple interested in you as a writer, they want to read what you have written. These are your fans.

Here's the drawback to selling to your friends: They may not want to read your book. It's a fact. The reasons may vary, they may not like the genre you have written your book for, they may not even like to read, or they just might not have the time to read your book unless it is totally relevant to them. Don't be disappointed or discouraged when the response you get from your friends and family is not what you expected. Your readers will find you in other ways.

One way to overcome this drawback to selling to your friends is to offer them a free copy. Yes, that's right. A free copy. Not to all of them of course, you would go broke. Giveaways are great ways to get readers.

Talk to them. Make a personal connection. Call them or talk to them face to face.

Everyone wants to know you care. They want to know if you are personally vested in them, in your friendship or relationship with them. Until the fact that you care about them is a reality to them you do not have the right to present your book to them. You can ask for a favor from them but why would they do that for you if they have not heard from you in months or even years?

Just because you published a book and need readers does not give you the right to dig up old friendships and ask for favors before you have reconnected. And don't get reconnected just because you need or want them to read your book. That is not playing fair. They will feel used. You don't need that kind of negative energy in your life and they don't either. Connect but do it because you genuinly like and care about the one you are trying to connect with. We all have friends that we have not talke to in a very long time. Reconnecting is normal.

If you try to connect with them on Facebook first or on Twitter or any of the other Social Networks you have lost the personal touch. It's the voice, the tone, the words, it's caring enough to call them or ask them to have a cup of coffee with you that means you think enough of them to take the time and to make the effort to connect with them. It makes them feel special. Wouldn't it make you feel special? Like they cared? That's the feeling you are going for. That's the type of connection you want to make. A personal one. A real one. Connect soon.

Connect Using Social Media

You want to take advantage of every opportunity to get as many readers as you can. One great way to do this is to use Social Media. It is a very important tool in your tool box as an authorpreneur. That's right, you are now in business for yourself promoting your book in every way you can.

When I finished writing my first book I had no idea that I would then have to learn to sell it myself. I just never thought that far ahead. Perhaps you did and you're off to a good start. A better start than I was. So use social media to get the word out about your book. Don't use social media as a way to "sell" your books. Instead, use it to let people know where they can buy one. Your job is to let people know about your book. What's in it for them? How will they benefit? Why should they invest both their time and their money in your book? Create some buzz! Create some interest in your book.

Let social "media" do it's job. The job of media is to inform. To let people know what's happening and where. The who, what, when, where, why, and how of things. Use this to your advantage. Get help from Fiverr.com if you are not sure how all that social media stuff works. For example, you can use quotes from your book on Facebook and guide them to your book with links.

Create an Online Presence

 Facebook is one of the best ways to keep in touch with family and friends. Be mindful of the time you spend on Facebook, you need to spend your time writing your next book! Seriously, don't try to sell your book. Make friends, give som books away, but be sure to let them know about your book. Give them some details and always share the link where you book can be puchased.

 Twitter is a great way to send short news blurbs, quotes, updates on you and on your book. You are an author. People are more interested in you than in your book. They want to know what you are doing and thinking

 Linkedin is a professional network. Everyone needs a Linkedin account. Create your account and tell others about your skills, who knows what connections you'll find over there. Just remember this group is for businesses and professionals seeking employment or networking.

These are the main three Social Networking sites.

Of course there are others that I will just mention and list here for you:

http://www.Pinterest.com
http://www.YouTube.com
http://www.instagram.com
http://www.googleplus.com
http://www.tumblr.com

These are the top 7 social networking sites according to ebizMBA Inc. Each one recieving over 100,000,000 unique hits per month.

http://www.ebizmba.com/articles/social-networking-websites

The Second Income Stream:
Sell to Brick and Morter Bookstores

As a Beauty Consultant for Mary Kay Cosmetics I learned the value of positive statements like, **"If it is to be, it is up to me."** This is the truth. Mary Kay and all the other successful people in life take the time to learn to be successful. You should to. If you want to be a successful authorpreneur that is. If not, stop here and read no further. It will be a waste of our time! If you want to be successful, read on. I have much more to share with you.

Since I use CreateSpace I am familiar with what they offer. My books are on Amazon.com which is the world's largest book selling company in the world. They help your books sell through their advertising methods. This is still not enough though. Your book could sit there like a little fish in a big ocean waiting for someone to drop you some bait. Or you can be like a more agressive shark and go after what you want. YOU need to get your book "out there" to the readers who want to read the book you have written. They are there! It is up to you to find out where they are. Many of them frequent bookstores.

Selling in bookstores is not that difficult. It is however time consuming. You will have to weigh the options for yourself and figure out if the time you exert will equal to the sales you will make.

Bookstores have overhead. The expenses they must have each month must be met in order for them to stay in business. They will usually take your book and put them on their shelves for 40 to 60 percent of sales. This is the average wholesale price.

Taking your book to the bookstore yourself is the best way to do business with local and regional bookstores. Keep in mind the amount of time and gas you will spend to get your books into the bookstores.

Let me help you make a few decisions about selling in book stores in bookstores, or not, by asking you a few directed questions. Your answers to the questions will give you insight into your goals for your book. It's your book, they are your goals.

Questionairre for Selling to Book Stores

1. What is your motivation for selling your book?
Money? Then you will probably want to sell everywhere you can.
Fame? The PR for book signings will help you gain recognition
To Help Others? Another great reason to get the book everywhere.

2. Are you busy?
How busy are you?
Do you have time to go ask a bookstore to sell your book for you?
Are you available for book signings at bookstores?
Do you have a family that still requires your help?

3. How much time are you willing to invest in selling your book?
Are you willing to invest 10 hours a week?
Are you willing to invest 2?
Are you willing to become a full-time authorpreneur?
Do you manage your time well?
Are you willing to manage your time so you can be successful?

4. Do you have the skills you need to sell your book?
Are you good at sales?
Are you shy and timid or are you a people person?
How much time are you willing to invest in learning the skills you
    need?

5. Are you good with cover designs, creating marketing materials, computers, graphic design, scheduling, promoting yourself?
You will need to be all those things or you will
    need to hire help. Help is not always cheap
    or easy to come by. Look at Fiverr.com for
    help first.

Self publishing is not for everyone. Really look at
your lifestyle. Is is worth doing all the selling yourself?
Your other option is to go with a traditional publisher.
Writing the book was the easy part for me. Getting it
into the bookstores, selling it, getting the word out about
the book, that's the hard part.

Top 14 Bookstore Chains in the USA

According to Wikipedia here is a list of bookstores listed in the USA. You can access the links to each bookstore by following this link to their website: https://en.wikipedia.org/wiki/List_of_bookstore_chains#United_States

Barnes & Noble
Book Off USA
Books-A-Million
Deseret Book
Family Christian Stores
Follett's
Half Price Books
Hastings Entertainment
Hudson News
Joseph-Beth Booksellers
LifeWay Christian Resources
Powell's Books
Schuler Books & Music
Books, Inc.

You are not limited to the bookstores in the USA. You can sell your books to other English speaking countries. You can even get your book translated into other languages and sell them in nonEnglish speaking countries.

Most bookstores are stocked with the new books published traditionlly. However, indie authors are springing up by the thousands and we are becomeing a voice to be reckoned with. Many have hit the bestseller's list and their books have sold millions of copies. You can do the same thing they have done.

All it takes is a little hard work, some determination, and a lot of time and of course some skills. However, you can always outsource and hire someone to help.

Contact Info for the Five Top Bookstores

Barnes & Noble
This is the link for you to learn how to sell at B&N
https://help.barnesandnoble.com/app/publisher_author/list/session/L3Rp
bWUvMTQ1OTMzMjgzNC9zaWQvMm56VkRMTW0%3D

Books-A-Million
This link is for publishers. I suggest if you are serious about writing and ublishing books you write several of them and have your own publishing company as I mentioned earlier.
http://www.booksamillion.com/publishers/coop.html?
id=6593330156620#marketing

Family Christian Stores
This link gives you all the details you need for publishing a Christian book. http://www.familychristian.com/productreview

Hastings Entertainment
Hastings will hold book signings for local authors and sell a few books. Contact local stores https://www.gohastings.com/custserv/custserv.jsp?
pageName=hastings_store_locator

LifeWay Christian Resources
Here's the link for product submission information
https://support.lifeway.com/app/answers/detail/a_id/324/
session/L3RpbWUvMTQ0MTIyNjI1NS9zaWQvVzJRNH
Z1dm0%3D

You are not limited to the bookstores in the USA. You can sell your books to other English speaking countries. You can even get your book translated into other languages and sell them in nonEnglish speaking countries.

Most bookstores are stocked with the new books published traditionlly. However, indie authors are springing up by the thousands and we are becomeing a voice to be reckoned with. Many have hit the bestseller's list and their books have sold millions of copies. You can do the same thing they have done. All it takes is a little hard work, some determination, and a lot of time.

Income Stream
Number Three

The Third Income Stream: Specialized Groups

With this option, selling your printed book to specialized groups, you have more opportunities than you do with the top bookstore chains. Often they will not receive books from Indie authors like you and I. This means we need to get a little more creative when it comes to creating income with our printed book.

Here are a few suggestions.

1. Schools
   - Age appropriate books can be placed in school libraries.
2. University Libraries
3. Day Care Centers
   - You can do a reading. Perhaps parents will purchase your book.
4. Youth oriented groups
5. Boys or Girls Clubs
6. Public Libraries
   Here is a link that will help you sell your book to a library
   http://www.ala.org/tools/libfactsheets/alalibraryfactsheet05
7. Profesionals
   - Is your book's topic targeted to a profession? Medical professionals? Stay at home moms? Lawyers? College Students?
8. Small Groups
   - Church groups, Mothers Against Drunk Drivers, Suicide Prevention, Boy Scouts, Girl Scount, etc.
9. Senior Citizen Groups
   - AARP, etc.
10. National Organizations
    - like the one for the Reform of Marijuana Laws, the Christian Coalition of America, American Humane Society, or the National Foreign Trade Counsel

You have a voice. Make it count where it matter the most. What platform would that be for your book? The different types of groups available to you are virtually unlimited! Use your imagination! Find your niche' (that area or group of people you can impact with your book).

Go here for many more ideas: http://votesmart.org/interest-groups#.Vyro7_krKUk

Speaking at Specialized Groups

Ok!! I heard that gasp of air. I felt the hair stand up on the back of your neck. Scared? Of course you are. Public Speaking is the number one fear. Dr. Glen Croston has some interesting points. Perhaps if you undestand the root of the fear from a primal origion you can begin to overcome your fears enough to actually speak in public.

Dr. Glen Croston said, " Our fear of standing up in front of a group and talking is so great that we fear it more than death, in surveys at least" (Croston, 2012). He goes on to explain that people had to "collaborate" to survive. Croston said, "Humans survived by their wits and their ability to collaborate" (Croston 2012). Failure to be accepted meant you got "ostracized" or kicked out of the social group. This doomed the one without protection. So therefore, we fear public speaking more than death because to be rejected is to be doomed. Croston links the fears.

My personal take on the matter, face your fears. Think in terms of "What is the worst possible scenerio?" If the worst if death then I'm ok! LOL Seriously, public speaking is not that deadly. In fact, once you get the anxiety in check (it never really goes away) you might even have some fun.

Find some local groups that you can speak at. Schools, Lion's Club, Men or Women's groups, etc. Ask around for ideas from others. Then talk to the ones you want to meet with and share with them the information about your book to see if it will be a good fit for you both. If you have written a book about chickens then you don't have much of an audience at a ladies tea or a men's group that raises funds for children. But, you would have a great audience with Homesteaders, homeschoolers, survivalists, farmers both large scale and small scale. You could put posters up at farm and tractor supply stores, and you could put posters or even have your books for sale at feed stores, or anywhere they sold chickens.

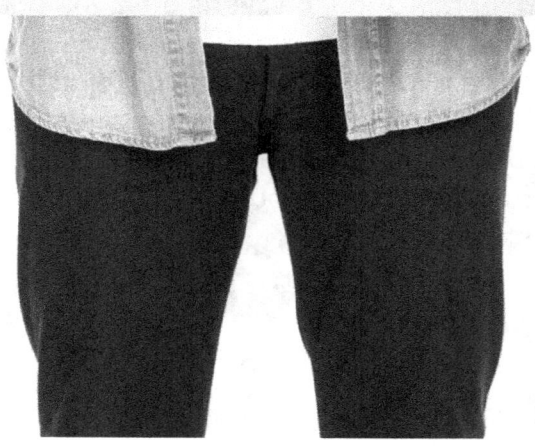

How to Have a Successful Book Signing

Successful book signings do not just happen. They take a little work on your part. The colors on your table matter! See the green tablecloth under the books. It does not distract but provides the eye with something a little darker to land on. Notice there are two books on stand plus a poster which is standing. All for visual effect.

The tables are usually right in the front of the store so you get to greet everyone that walks in the day you are there. If you are a bit introverted this may prove to be a worthwhile challenge that I believe you are ready and more than able to handle. Practice greeting people and being friendly when you go shopping, when you buy gas, when you go out to eat, you can greet people everywhere you go! And people like to be greeted, especially with a friendly face.

To have a successful book signing you need to plan ahead. Create business cards with your book cover on the front and the website where they can purchase your book on the back. Create some bookmarkers as give-aways with your book cover on the front and your contact information on the back. Even create some postcards to give out and to mail out. The more marketing materials you have the better of you are.

Have FUN!!!

My first book, my first book signing at Hastings.

Income
Stream
Number
Five

Income Stream Number Five:
Sell Your Printed Book Online

If you published your book through CreateSpace you are already selling your book online through Amazon.com. CreateSpace.com is an Amazon company. I do hope you are taking advantage of the optional distribution channels. You can choose to publish through the standard option of Amazon.com, Amazon Europe, and CreatSpace eStore. The Expanded Distribution, which is now free, includes bookstores and online retailers, libraries and academic institutions, and CreateSpace Direct. All this for free. I personally took advantage of everything they had to offer.

Be aware though, that to take advantage of all the distribution channels some require you to have a CreatSpace.com assigned ISBN number. This is actually not a problem because you still retain all the rights to your book.

Taking advantage of selling your book online through CreateSpace.com makes good sense. There are still things you need to do. To think that it is enough to have your book available online at Amazon.com is selling you and your book short and may take years for your book to sell very many copies. This will not make you much money is royalties.

Five Additional Ways
to Sell Your Printed Book Online

1. Do a book tour.

You can do a regional book tour if finances are an issue. Stay in your local area. Do a tour and set a perimeter of a 50 mile radius. Or a 100 mile radius. You set your own limits. The more bookstores you tour, the more books you will sell.

2. Get Interviews on the Radio

Local radio stations may feature you as a local author. Do a search online for an Internet radio program that interviews Indie authors and narrow it down by searching for programming that suits your genre.

3. Host a Book Launching Party

Invite your friends and ask them to bring a friend. If they do they get a free book! Make it fun.

4. Be a Guest on Someone's Podcast

This is similar to being interviewed on the radio, but the audience has been built up to the info presented in the podcast. They are typically targeted subjects.

5. Get on TV for an interview

This may intimidate you. It does me. But it is a guaranteed way for people to find out about your book. Exposure equals sales. Especially if you have a good story surrounding your book.

Bibliography

Rosenthal, M. (2011). Book sales statistics. Retrieved on March 14, 016
from http://www.fonerbooks.com/booksale.htm

About the Author

Cindy Hyde is an author, ordained minister, pastoral counselor, certified professional life coach, and CEO and founder of The East Texas Healing Center. Over the course of her career, Cindy has become known as a trusted partner among those who are serious about overcoming life's struggles. Few things bring her more satisfaction that helping people overcome those struggles, and she has been so blessed to work with hundreds of individuals who are anxious to maximize their potential, confidence, and sense of self-worth.

As someone who has forced herself to overcome great tragedy, loss, and obstacles in her own life, Cindy carries deep empathy and compassion for those who have suffered as she has, and she is ready to help shoulder the burden of anyone who comes to her for help.

Cindy is the author of numerous books, including Making Peace With Your Past: One Choice at a Time; External Scars from Internal Wounds; Beyond Abuse: A Journey of Restoration; A Woman of Acts; and Prisoners of War Shackled No More. Cindy holds a master's degree in adult education and training, a bachelor's degree in communication, and an associate's degree in visual communication from the University of Phoenix.

When she's not in the office or with clients, Cindy loves traveling, sharing her message with others, and spending time with friends and family. She currently lives in Nacogdoches, TX with her wonderful husband, Michael. Learn more about Cindy by visiting her website at www.fiverr.com/cindyhyde

Also by Author

A Woman of Acts

A Workbook for Writers Who Want to Be Authors or Authorpreneurs

External Scars from Internal Wounds

Following Ancient Paths: A Chronological Study of 52 Ancient Biblical Stories

How to Create Multiple Income Streams with One Book

Making Peace with Your Past: One Choice at a Time

Prisoners of War Shackled No More

Social Media Marketing for Authors, Entrepreneurs and Ministers

Wisdom from My Heart

Cindy's books are available on Amazon, Barnes and Noble, Kindle, and cindyhyde.com

Contact the Author

Cindy Hyde, MA

CindyHyde.com
875 CR 811
Nacogdoches, TX 75961
936-221-0838

Facebook: cindylhyde
Twitter: @cindyhyde

eMail: cindylhyde@gmail.com